style to go | Decorating

D0064270

style to go

Decorating

JOSH GARSKOF

The Taunton Press

The Taunton Press
Inspiration for hands-on living®

The Taunton Press, Inc., 63 South Main Street,
PO Box 5506, Newtown, CT 06470-5506
e-mail: tp@taunton.com

Jacket/Cover design: Allison Wilkes
Interior design: Kimberly Adis, Allison Wilkes
Layout: Kimberly Adis

Library of Congress Cataloging-in-Publication Data
Garskof, Josh.
   Style to go-- decorating / Josh Garskof.
      p. cm.
   ISBN-13: 978-1-56158-934-0
   ISBN-10: 1-56158-934-9
   1. Interior decoration. I. Title. II. Title: Style to go. III.
Title: Decorating.

NK2115.G316 2007
747--dc22
                                    2006020156

Printed in China
10 9 8 7 6 5 4 3 2 1

The following manufacturers/names appearing in *Decorating* are
trademarks: Alkco® Lighting, American Standard®, Bed, Bath &
Beyond®, Blanco®, California Closets®, Casabella®, Chicago Faucets®,
ClosetMaid®, Corian®, Country Floors®, Dacor®, Elkay®, Exposures®,
Filofax®, Franke® Sinks & Faucets, Freedom Bag®, Frigidaire®,
Frontgate®, General Electric®, Halo® Lighting, Hold Everything®, Ikea®,
Jenn-Air®, KitchenAid®, Kmart™, Kohler® Plumbing, Kraftmaid®,
Levenger®, Lightolier®, Maytag®, Moen®, Restoration Hardware℠,
Rubbermaid®, Target®, Thermador®, Thermos®, Tupperware®, Umbra®,
Viking®, Wicanders® Cork Flooring, Wolf®.

contents

color

Shifting the color from one wall to the next can add a feeling of depth to a space because each surface takes on its own identity.

Left Green
painted trim and
a light wood desk
carry the colors
of nature into this
sunny office.

Right Purple walls
and a painted-
green dresser
took their color
cues from a
simple flower
bouquet.

Mother Nature, such as beige sand with foliage, or cobalt sky with white clouds.

Create the right mood with color.

Blue relaxes and refreshes.

Yellow increases energy and lifts spirits.

Orange encourages conversation.

Red stimulates the appetite.

Green refreshes and soothes.

Wallpaper with vertical stripes lends height to this dining room while also eliminating the need for art on every wall.

Create stripes using paint
instead of wallpaper to
make future color changes easier.

Horizontal stripes
visually lower a
high ceiling, making
a room feel more
intimate.

The relaxed mood of this green bathroom is enhanced by the addition of only one other color—white—which is used for the cabinets, fixtures, and trim.

Red is flattering to most skin tones, so it's perfect for a bathroom.

Small rooms seem
larger when given
a muted palette.
Linen wall paint,
cherry trim, and
beige faux-stone
porcelain tile
extend throughout
this home.

Save yourself from having to repaint whenever you redecorate. Choose a neutral paint palette and introduce color with easy-to-change furnishings.

Top Using rich colors on walls won't make the space feel small if you keep the ceiling pure white, which visually lifts it.

Bottom Light pink would have made this bedroom more serene, but the fuchsia walls appealed to this bedroom's pre-teen occupant. The pale bed linens help to soften the effect.

The bold colors of the couch, rug, and throw pillows prevent the intense turquoise walls from overpowering the room.

Who says a wall can be only one color? Glazing involves overlaying two paints—either close in value or with a high contrast. Paint stores sell DIY kits.

Paint mismatched
furniture a single color
to unify the pieces
and make them feel like
a coordinated set.

Fabrics are usually chosen to comple-ment the permanent features of a room, but in this case the fruit print on a favorite sofa (top) inspired a hand-painted tile backsplash (bottom).

The upholstery fabric and Venetian glass lamp in this living room were carefully selected to pick up the colors in the space's showpiece, a painting of a busy kitchen.

Busy wallpaper
and upholstery
patterns call for
something plain,
or at least neutral, for the
window treatments.

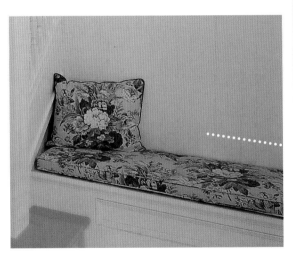

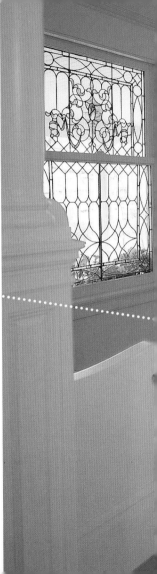

Painted stairs lend drama to a foyer, entryway, or landing. The colors of the alternating yellow risers and green treads continue in a diamond checkerboard on the adjacent floor. The fabric of the bench cushion contains both colors and ties the floor and walls together.

Combine a mix
of textures,
from wall tile to
plush surfaces
to glossy cabinets,
to enliven
the colors
of a room.

A red and green color scheme won't look
like Christmas if you choose the right hues.

Left Tucked into a narrow passageway between two bedrooms, this home office feels bright and cheery thanks to a yellow and white paint scheme.

Right When a single color is used for every wall surface—including trim and window mullions—furnishings will become the focal points of the space.

What makes this relatively monochromatic color scheme work is the appealing variety of textures, from the smooth wood tabletop to the coarse sisal rug and velvety upholstery.

Orange and hot pink may seem like risky color choices, but they can bring a splash of warmth and vibrancy to a home.

A mix of patterns
looks best when
they share a color palette,
as evidenced here by
the combination of
reds, blues, and yellows.

To create an intimate space in a long hallway, a colorful rug and sofa were used to carve out a distinct zone.

Red is the primary color in this bedroom, but the blue floor, shams, and blanket keep the bold hue from being overpowering.

Think outside the box spring.

If you don't like the look of bed skirts, cover your box spring with an extra fitted sheet.

Soft, neutral hues create a relaxing bedroom environment. To keep things from becoming boring, a bold floral print has been added in small doses.

Top Color can set the mood of a room. The sunflower walls in this living room create a sunny disposition while the red in the dining room has a more formal feel.

Left Don't be afraid of color. Even a mix of blue seating pieces, green window treatments, and purple walls can create a successful effect.

Top One small strip of color can be enough to create a focal point within a spacious room as with the bar area in this game room.

Left A great way to create intimate zones within a larger space is to change paint color. This sitting area is immediately identified by the orange wall.

Pastels are no longer restricted to the nursery.
Just feature something in the room in a stronger tone
(such as the headboard at left), to draw the eye in.
If you use strong colors in a kid's room keep
something neutral, such as the floor covering,
to offer a resting point.

furniture

These sophisticated armchairs have a playful feel thanks to the unusual print on the upholstery fabric.

Finding new uses for old things is a sure way to create a one-of-a-kind look.

An old cornmeal chest needed little besides a good cleaning to anchor a country style vignette.

Console tables are most commonly used in hallways and behind sofas, but their narrow profiles also make them useful writing desks in small spaces.

When you're looking for attractive furniture at a bargain price, go for pieces with simple styling because they tend to age gracefully.

Make your furniture fit your style by choosing just the right upholstery fabric instead of what happens to be displayed on the salesroom floor.

Left Nesting tables need not be completely stowed away when you're not using them. Try arranging them in a telescoping pattern to give them more visual impact in the room.

Right A comfortable quilted chair and footstool turn a back hall into a cozy reading corner.

Right Though they look like standard over-stuffed armchairs, the plush seats in this living room swivel, allowing family members to turn toward conversation, a crackling fire, or the television inside the armoire.

Bottom No eat-in kitchen? Furnish your dining room with a table and chairs that you can either dress up for formal meals or dress down for casual ones.

A cushioned bench placed just inside the front entrance will subtly encourage guests to remove their shoes.

Protect your carpets
by wearing slippers
around the house
to prevent outdoor grit and grime
from getting tracked on them.

There is harmony in this bedroom thanks to the cool, complementary colors of the furniture and accessories.

Looking for an area rug that fits your color scheme and your floor space?

Purchase a wall-to-wall remnant, and have it bound to the exact size you need.

Wicker furniture is casual and inviting regardless
of the setting; the carved wooden table and topiary
plant carry out the nature theme.

Let the **colors and textures of houseplants shine** by cleaning them in the sink or shower with a hand-held sprayer on the gentle setting.

Paired with understated wood furnishings, the coral and white slipcovers, drapes, and chair cushions combine to provide strong color. Visual interest is provided by the change from large stripe to small to diagonal.

There's beauty in the shape of functional furnishings. Red welting highlights the form of a sofa, while the dark tones of the two armless chairs give them bold silhouettes against the light background.

Understated white furniture is counterbalanced by yellow walls and a sisal rug, both of which are neutral enough to maintain the urbane look while still offering a tonal contrast.

A pair of square red benches provides seating in this compact living room, where full-sized chairs or a loveseat would have created a traffic jam.

A sectional sofa will provide the maximum seating capacity for any L- or U-shaped furniture configuration.

Tired of your furniture but don't want to spend lots of money on new stuff? Make a quick décor change by purchasing ready-made slipcovers that can be "custom fitted" by adjusting an elastic edge or bow tie.

White slipcovers have a crisp, summery feel. When cooler weather returns, they can be removed (and washed) to expose the colorful fabrics underneath.

Mid-century modern furnishings are affordable, comfortable, and trendy. Bent plywood chairs and a simple molded pedestal table (left) offer a light-hearted, light-colored, and lightweight look. And a 1950s Streamline shelf (above) displays a collection of glass and ceramics from the era.

Mismatched dining room chairs can work together as long as they have a unifying theme, in this case the wicker from which they're made.

Because the architecture of this space is so strong, the table and chairs were kept simple.

Small rooms can look good with large-scale furnishings

as long as they aren't low to the ground or heavy.

Glass-topped tables and elevated sofa legs invite the eye to look past furnishings, so they take up almost no visual space and make the room feel larger.

This pair of small coffee tables can be moved to wherever
they're needed during parties, and because they're the
darkest objects in the decorating scheme, they help to
focus attention on appetizers and conversation.

Audio equipment is hidden behind the wood doors in this entertainment center thanks to a radio-frequency remote control.

Small spaces require furniture that can do double-duty.

Left To provide table-top space for everything from reading glasses to glasses of water, a nightstand should be no more than 2 in. higher or lower than the top of your mattress.

Right Nesting tables provide extra surfaces that can be moved anywhere in the room as needed.

Top A wicker bench helps to prevent this large bedroom from feeling too expansive—and it provides a more comfortable spot for getting dressed than the high mattress.

Right A canopy bed is a good choice for a room with vaulted ceilings because it helps to fill the vertical space and keep the room from seeming empty.

The key to decorating a large multipurpose space is to use the furnishings to create distinct "rooms," such as the television, dining, and sitting areas in this great room, and to repeat decorative elements throughout the space.

Top Large floor pillows are a versatile addition to a family room, offering extra seating, a place to curl up on the floor, and a totally mobile design element.

Right Eye-catching contrasts don't have to involve color. These tables combine the opposing textures of rough rattan and smooth leather—and their very shapes are a study in dissimilarity.

End tables can take many shapes and forms. Most important when choosing one is to be sure it provides enough surface space, is at the right height, and is sturdy enough for whatever it will be supporting.

PIRANESI

window
treatments

When this curtain is open, natural light streams through the windows and headboard. When closed, the fabric's backing completely darkens the room for an afternoon nap.

Swing-away curtain
rods allow the occupant
of this cozy street-facing
window seat to choose
privacy or a chance to
gaze upon the world
outside.

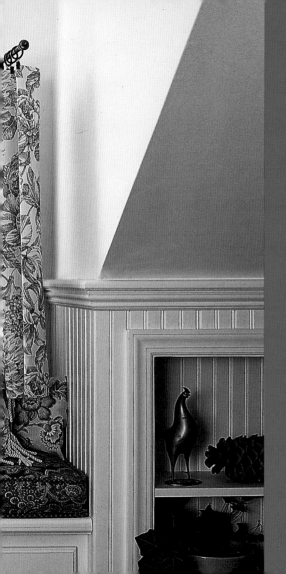

Louvered interior shutters screen direct sunlight while allowing breezes to flow through the window.

Treatments on doors should add blend in with treatments on windows

Left Roman shades work well on doors since they can be set at any height when not fully lowered for privacy.

Right Draperies aren't only for windows. They can cover French doors or entire walls of glass, softening the feel of the room and adding a striking design element.

their own style to the room but also to give the room a cohesive feel.

Bamboo shades lend
contrasting texture
to a room made up
of mostly solids and
neutrals.

Some curtains never close, so hang a single sheer panel behind them to improve your privacy. You'll still have your views, but it'll be a little harder to see into your windows from outside.

Simple valances dress up large windows without obstructing the view—and they hide the room-darkening shades installed behind them.

Roman shades combine the tailored look of a fitted shade with the decorative effect of attention-grabbing fabric.

Here's a simple way to make your own curtain. Sew a satin ribbon along the top edge of a favorite print that's been hemmed to size and add ribbon tie tops every 6 in.

The combination of two fabrics give this swag-and-jabot window dressing a casual flair while complementing the colors of the accessories.

Simple white-painted curtain rods
can be found in your local home
center. These mimic the shape of
the finial on the bedpost.

Poles, finials, and tie-backs are available in a wide range of styles and finishes. Matching the pole to the finial creates a seamless line, while mixing finishes will draw attention to the finials.

Plastic hoops inserted between panels of fabric add the finishing touch to a retro-styled room.

When used sparingly, bold colors like red add energy to a room without overpowering it.

Decorative accents, like fringe trim, ribbon banding, and tassels, can add texture and style to any window treatment.

Top This small room benefits from having no window treatment and only painted trim to call attention to the window. Curtains would have made the room feel even more closed in.

Right If a view is important, let the window treatments take a backseat. These drapes all but disappear into the white window trim.

It's easier for guests
to find fresh towels
and washcloths
if they're stored
on open shelves
rather than behind
closed doors.

stylish
storage

The wire grid sold at home centers offers a simple way to amp up the storage capacity of any kitchen. A store employee can cut it to size and suggest the right hooks for hanging pots, pans, and other cooking gear.

Storing pots, pans,
and tools in plain sight
highlights their beauty—
and conserves space.

To hide this well-stocked home office, its slide-out work surface and rolling printer table stow behind the closet doors. The comfy chair, however, stays out to become a handy bedroom seat.

Unused space under stairs is the perfect place for coats, boots, and umbrellas. Treated with the same paneling and baseboard as the walls, this one practically vanishes when the door is closed.

Your junk drawer probably doesn't look quite like this, but it can. Install full-extension drawer glides and use plastic containers to create individual compartments for all of your supplies.

Make the most of every space by tucking in shelves and wall-hung storage units on empty walls. This solution also keeps baking needs right at hand.

Left Welcoming entries provide a place for coats and hats. Simple storage accessories can be found at most home stores and installed in a flash.

Right Cubbies like these are great for storing outdoor gear— for people and pets—but you can also use wire shelving or ready-to-assemble components.

stylish storage 121

Top Instead of a stationary table near this door, a rolling cart allows drinks and food to be easily moved outdoors.

Right Use the same material for different elements in a room to unify the space and add surprise. You have to look closely to see that a dressing room is hidden behind panels of fabric.

Install full-extension roll-out shelves in kitchen cabinets to get the most from them.

A cookbook shelf mounted high on the wall makes good use of otherwise empty space.

found
space

This sunny spot was planned as an informal dining area, but the view is so nice that the owners turned it into a sitting area that they can enjoy whenever they want.

Want your finished basement to have the warmth and sophistication of wood floors?

Install laminate flooring, which looks like the real thing, but is cheaper, easier to install, and, is approved for below-ground use.

For this basement apartment, petite wall cabinets were tucked under the high windows and the ceiling fan was recessed into the drop ceiling to prevent it from looming too low over the chef.

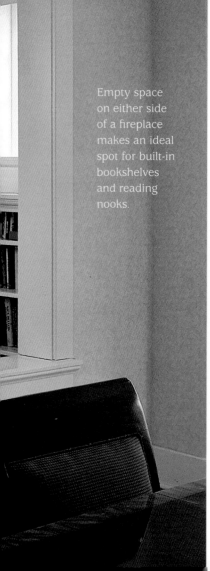

Empty space on either side of a fireplace makes an ideal spot for built-in bookshelves and reading nooks.

Open shelving turns everyday cooking tools into an attractive display while helping to keep a compact kitchen feeling as spacious as possible.

With the sink instead of the cooktop in the island, there's no need for a bulky vent hood in the middle of the kitchen, leaving room for a unique ceiling-hung shelf for displaying pottery.

Almost every house has a small nook, alcove, or dormer
that's basically wasted space. Install a window seat and
it'll become a favorite spot to hang out.

This home office is tucked entirely into a former closet, so it disappears when the doors are shut.

Transforming space can be simple.
This alcove would have worked just as
well with a chair and book-rack
instead of bench and built-in shelf.

Top Because a screened porch already has a floor and roof, enclosing it requires minimal construction work—and offers a great way to add a home office, den, or playroom.

Left Pocket doors save space because there's no need to keep the adjacent walls clear for the doors to swing open.

kid-friendly décor

A cushioned bench makes an ideal addition to a young child's room because it offers a comfortable seat, a playing surface, and plenty of storage that's within her reach.

Good students all have one thing in common: A dedicated and well-organized place to do their work.

Make doing homework more fun by having kids make the space their own.

·······

Hang artwork and photos.

·······

Group supplies
in colorful containers.

·······

Add baskets or a
rolling cart with drawers
to help keep things organized.

Dual sinks ease the morning routine when brothers or sisters share a bathroom. The children can also have their own drawers and cabinets.

Alphabet decorations bring youthful whimsy to family rooms without making the décor off-putting to grownups.

This room's sea-life motif came from easy-to-find crafts supplies. The curtain tie-backs were made with preserved starfish and hot glue and the wall images were created using simple rubber stamps and paint.

Relax and put your feet up.

every armchair

Pillows add a new dimension to family space. These work double-duty as back rests on chairs or floor pillows.

Unless it reclines,
needs a foot stool or ottoman.

A throw pillow provides a splash of color for neutral colored armchairs and sofas.

A little color goes a long way—and infuses
fun and a kid-like atmosphere to any room.

Storage systems
needn't be elabo-
rate. Transparent
boxes help kids
see what's inside.

Give an old wood floor new life by painting it. In a room without much décor, this floor is the focal point.

Don't take the shotgun approach to finding studs in the wall when you're hanging heavy objects. Purchase an electronic stud finder and you'll hit them on the first try every time.

Small store-bought shelves like these can be hung on virtually any wall to instantly create a charming spot for supplies or decorations.

Painted pegboard, which is inexpensive and can be found at your local home center, can transform a plain wall into a storage area for craft supplies.

Top Families can co-exist in harmony when spaces accommodate the needs of adult and child, as evidenced in this kitchen for a mom who loves to cook and keep her kids close.

Left Young kids need nearly constant attention and supervision, so the ideal spot for a play room is right next to the kitchen.

This bathroom comes to life thanks to the vibrant colors. The old tub was repainted when the space was being remodeled.

Kids' artwork adds to the informality of this long hallway. The art, window seat, and bookshelves all invite family members to stop and linger as they walk through their home.

decorative
details

Here's an ever-changing
display that will brighten
any kitchen: Just fill a
decorative bowl or basket
with whatever produce
happens to be in season
at the moment.

A collection of paintings completely fills this living room wall without over-powering the space because the artwork shares a color palette, and the walls and ceiling pick up recurring hues.

Family photos look better when they're not just a bunch of snapshots stuck on the fridge. Load them into a set of matching frames with mats, and hang them together.

Add your personality to any small tabletop.

Fill an end table with framed family photos.

......

Add a large vase of fresh flowers.

......

Group together seashells or sea glass from your last beach vacation.

A woven wicker tray containing a thick picture book has been used to raise the level of this nightstand—and to keep small items from falling off the edge.

Art can be a harmonious grouping or an eclectic mix. Vintage tea canisters decorate a mantel top (above) and hand-glazed tiles hang gallery style above a tiled fireplace (right).

displayed as works of art.

Look for fun ways to make your decorations work together, such as this pairing of glass bottles with an abstract painting of what looks like bubbles floating up from their tops.

Glass canisters create unbeatable seals for keeping foodstuffs fresh—and they turn the wonderful colors and textures of essential ingredients into objets d'art.

Found objects, such as these metal pails, make unexpected containers for houseplants. And there's no need to drill holes in the bottoms. Simply drop already-potted plants into slightly larger decorative containers.

Take total control of your lighting
by replacing wall switches with dimmers.

Left These unshaded pendants offer a hip retro look thanks to their 19th-century-style bulbs, which are oversized and have a glowing carbon filament just like the ones in Thomas Edison's day.

Right These stained-glass pendants do just what they're supposed to—grab attention and add style.

Inspired by a vintage cooking range, this period kitchen has no upper cabinets. Instead, a subway-tile backsplash and metal shelving and hooks create an open, old-fashioned feel.

Top Decorations don't have to fit one single style. Here, a Moroccan screen, 1960s brass lamp, and California art pottery work together to create an eclectic look.

Left A bouquet of on-the-vine berries offers seasonal color during the winter months, harmonizing with the hues of the carpet, coffee-table runner, and throw blanket.

Before your guests arrive, don't forget to grab a bouquet of fresh flowers, which brings natural colors, energy, and aroma to the home.

Simple, understated bedding helps to tone down busy bedroom furnishings, from the carved bedposts to the kitschy mirrors and leopard print ottoman.

Lamp shades do a lot more than just hide bulbs and switches. They also diffuse the light and make it gentler on the eyes, as well as add a design element—either fabric, paper, or glass—to the décor.

Baskets of all
shapes and sizes
can be used for
decorative storage:

Clean towels
in the bathroom

......

Mail in the kitchen

......

Kids' books in
a playroom

......

Desk supplies
in a home office

The trio of botanical prints in this causal entryway help to break up the two-sided symmetry of a dual-drawer pine table with two storage baskets.

Any collection of objects can become an interesting display, from Thermos® bottles to mittens and gloves, snow globes, or antique glassware.

Open shelves in a kitchen create an ideal spot to add color with an eclectic dishware collection.

Get comfortable by choosing chairs
than the desk, countertop,

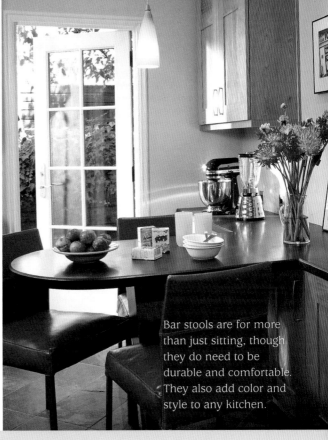

Bar stools are for more than just sitting, though they do need to be durable and comfortable. They also add color and style to any kitchen.

and stools that are exactly 12 in. lower or work surface they're paired with.

If you're positioning a mirror over a fireplace be sure it reflects something that's worth seeing twice.

This fireplace screen opens like a set of French doors when it's time to put another log on the fire and then closes securely for full coverage of the oversized fire box.

Multiple pieces of decorative
stone were used for the fireplace,
creating a wall of art that needs
little enhancement.

A storage bench and plenty of coat hooks—hung at adult and child heights—turn a back hall into an efficient mudroom.

Simple coat hooks paired with a chalkboard create an instant family message center.

A high shelf can resolve all sorts of decorating dilemmas, from where to display delicate collections that you don't want handled (above) to what to do with bookshelf speakers when there are no bookshelves in the room (right).

Shelves positioned high up on a wall should contain things you don't need to get down all too often but that doesn't mean they need to be a dumping ground for worn books and boxes of old photos.

Run out of wall space but not artwork? This shelf is filled with useful—and visually engaging—stuff.

If the bulletin board look isn't your style, add a fabric covering.

Sandwich corkboard between plywood and the fabric of your choice and use a staple gun to fasten the fabric to the back of the plywood.

Use corkboard as a wall covering in a home office or a message center and you'll always have a place to display everything from important reminders to family photographs and children's artwork.

Rummage through your attic or
to find old furniture then paint

Right This simple table gains a "shabby chic" appearance from a coat of white paint that was wiped away in some spots to let the blue underneath show through.

Left Cheerful checks, stripes, and polka-dots turn a simple dresser into the focal point of a boy's bedroom. The final touches are the painted lampshade and drawer pulls.

garage sales
it to give it new life.

Changing the knobs and pulls
screwdriver, and yet it totally

Knobs can be a focal point or blend in with their cabinetry. The Arts & Crafts style knobs and pulls complement the oak cabinets (bottom left).

on cabinetry is as easy as turning a changes the flavor of the cabinets.

decorative details

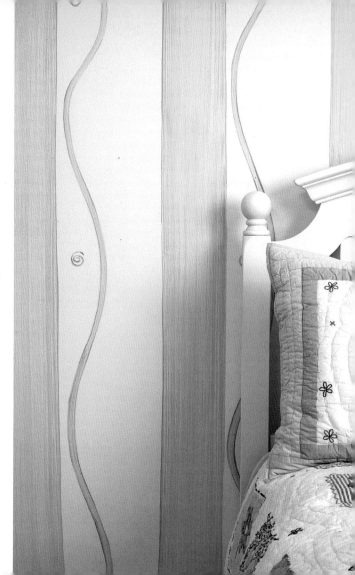

Right Simply
roll a colorful
coat of paint
over white and
then pull a dry
paint brush ver-
tically through it
while the paint
is wet to create
a strie pattern.

Left Combine
a painting tech-
nique like strie
with playful
details to create
a decorating
scheme in a
child's room.

With a little practice, it's easy to create appealing texture or pattern with paint.

sources

organizations

American Institute
of Architects (AIA)
1735 New York Ave. NW
Washington, DC 200006
www.aiaaccess.com

American Society of
Interior Designers (ASID)
608 Massachusetts Ave. NE
Washington, DC 20002
www.interiors.org

National Association of
Home Builders (NAHB)
1201 Fifteenth St. NW
Washington, DC 20005
www.nahb.org

National Association of
Professional Organizers
www.napo.net

National Association of the
Remodeling Industry (NARI)
4900 Seminary Road #3210
Alexandria, VA 22311
www.nari.org

National Kitchen & Bath
Association
687 Willow Grove St.
Hackettstown, NJ 07840
www.nkba.com

web sites

Decorating Den Interiors
www.decoratingden.com

Dr. Toy
www.drtoy.com

Energy Star
www.energystar.com/gov

Get Decorating
www.GetDecorating.com

HomePortfolio
www.homeportfolio.com

The Building and Home
Improvement Directory
www.build.com

U.S. Consumer Product
Safety Commission
www.cpsc.gov

product sources

Alkco® Lighting
www.alkco.com

American Standard®
www.americanstandard.com

Babybox.com
www.babybox.com

Bed, Bath & Beyond®
www.bedbathandbeyond.com

Bernhardt Furniture
Company
www.bernhardt.com

Blanco®
www.blancoamerica.com

Broadway Panhandler
www.broadwaypanhandler.com

Broyhill Furniture
Industries, Inc.
www.broyhillfurn.com

California Closets®
www.californiaclosets.com

Casabella®
www.casabella.com

CD Storehouse
(800) 829-4203

Chicago Faucets®
www.chicagofaucets.com

Closet Factory
www.closetfactory.com

ClosetMaid®
www.closetmaid.com

The Conran Shop
www.conran.com

The Container Store
www.containerstore.com

Corian®
www.corian.com

Crate & Barrel
www.crateandbarrel.com

Country Floors®
www.countryfloors.com

Dacor®
www.dacor.com

Design Within Reach
www.dwr.com

Elkay®
www.elkayusa.com

Exposures®
www.exposuresonline.com

Filofax®
www.filofax.com

Franke® Sinks & Faucets
www.frankeksd.com

Freedom Bag®
www.freedombag.com

Frigidaire®
www.frigidaire.com

Frontgate®
www.frontgate.com

General Electric®
www.geappliances.com

Graber Window Fashions
www.springs.com

Gracious Home
www.gracioushome.com

Harden Furniture, Inc.
www.harden.com

Halo® Lighting
www.cooperlighting.com

Hold Everything®
www.holdeverything.com

HomeDecInASec
www.homedecinasec.com

Ikea®
www.ikea.com

Jenn-Air®
www.jennair.com

KitchenAid®
www.kitchenaid.com

Kmart™
www.kmart.com

Knape & Vogt
www.knapeandvogt.com

Kohler® Plumbing
www.us.kohler.com

Kraftmaid®
www.kraftmaid.com

The Land of Nod
www.thelandofnod.com

Lamps Plus
www.lampsplus.com

Lane Home Furnishings
www.lanefurniture.com

Levenger®
www.levenger.com

Lightolier®
www.lightolier.com

Mannington, Inc.
www.mannington.com

Maytag®
www.maytag.com

Moen®
www.moen.com

Netkidswear.com
www.netkidswear.com

Poliform
www.poliformusa.com

Posh Tots
www.poshtots.com

Rejuvenation lighting
and hardware
www.rejuvenation.com

Restoration Hardware℠
www.restorationhardware.com

Rev-A-Shelf
www.rev-a-shelf.com

Rubbermaid®
www.rubbermaid.com

Seabrook Wallcoverings
www.seabrookwallcoverings.com

Serena & Lily
www.serenaandlily.com

Stacks and Stacks
www.stacksandstacks.com

Target®
www.target.com

Thermador®
www.thermador.com

Thomasville Furniture
Industries
www.thomasville.com

Tupperware®
www.tupperware.com

Umbra®
www.umbra.com

Velux America, Inc.
www.veluxusa.com

Vermont Soapstone Company
www.vermontsoapstone.com

Viking®
www.vikingrange.com

WallCandy Arts
www.wallcandyarts.com

Wallies
www.wallies.com

The Warm Biscuit Bedding Company
www.warmbiscuit.com

Wicanders® Cork Flooring
www.wicanders.com

Wolf®
www.subzero.com/wolf

York Wallcoverings
www.yorkwall.com

photo credits

pp. ii-iii: Photo: © Susan Gilmore.

p. v: (left) Photo: © Tria Giovan; (middle) Photo: © Wendell T. Webber; (right) Photo: © Eric Roth, Design: Susan Sargent.

p. vi: (far left & left) Photos: © Ken Gutmaker; (middle) Photo: © Jessie Walker; (right) Photo: © Jeremey Samuelson.

p. 1: (left) Photo: © Ken Gutmaker; (middle) Photo: courtesy The Land of Nod; (right) Photo: © Kari Haaviston, Design: Victoria Hagan.

CHAPTER 1

p. 3: Photo: © Ken Gutmaker.

p. 4: Photo: © Jamie Solomon.

p. 5: Photo © Eric Roth.

p. 7: Photo: © Ken Gutmaker.

p. 8: Photo © Rob Karosis.

p. 9: Photo: © Eric Piasecki.

pp. 10–11: Photos: © David Bravo.

p. 12: Photo: © Philip Clayton-Thompson.

p. 14: (top) Photo: © Rob Karosis; (bottom) Photo: © David Bravo.

p. 15: Photo: © Jennifer Cheung.

p. 16: Photos: © David Bravo.

p. 18: Photo: © Kathy Delwiler Lee.

p. 20: Photos: © Grey Crawford.

p. 21: Photo: Karen Tanaka, © The Taunton Press, Inc.

p. 22–23: Photo: © Alise O'Brien.

pp. 24–25: Photo: © Robert Perron.

pp. 26–27: Photo: © Jessie Walker.

p. 28: Photo: © Tria Giovan, Design: Mary Selover.

p. 29: Photo: © Tim Street-Porter, Design: Barbara Barry.

p. 30: Photo: © www.davidduncanlivingston.com.

p. 31: Photo: © Mark Samu, www.samustudios.com, Design: Eileen Kathryn Boyd Interiors.

p. 33: Photo: © Eric Roth, Design: Geyle Jerrey.

p. 34: Photo: © Eric Roth, Design: Susan Sargent.

p. 35: Photo: © Eric Roth, Design: Brad Morash.

pp. 36–37: Photo: © 2006 Carolyn L. Bates, www.carolynlbates.com.

p. 38: Photo: © Eric Roth, Design: Susan Sargent.

p. 39: Photo: © Tim Street-Porter.

p. 40: Photo: © Claudio Santini, Design: Linda Applewhite.

p. 41: Photo: © www.davidduncanlivingston.com.

p. 42: Photo: © Tim Street-Porter, Design: Jennifer Delonge.

p. 43: Photo: © Lisa Romerein.

CHAPTER 2

p. 45: Photo: © Ken Gutmaker.

p. 46: Photo: © Randy O'Rourke.

p. 48: Photo: © Rob Karosis.

p. 49: Photo: © colinmcguire.com.

p. 50: Photo: © Kari Haaviston, Design: James Biber for Pentagram Architects.

p. 51: Photo: © Randy O'Rourke.

p. 52: Photo: © Ellen Silverman.

p. 53: Photo: © Susan Gilmore.

p. 54: Photo: © Randy O'Rourke.

p. 56: Photo: © Mark Samu, www.samustudios.com, Design: Eileen Kathryn Boyd Interiors.

p. 58: Photo: © www.davidduncanlivingston.com.

pp. 60–62: Photos: © www.davidduncanlivingston.com.

p. 63: Photo: © Eric Roth, Design: Weena & Spook.

p. 64: Photo: © www.davidduncanlivingston.com.

p. 65: Photo: © Tim Street-Porter, Furniture Design: Roy McMakin.

p. 66: Photo: © www.davidduncanlivingston.com.

p. 68: Photo: © Tim Street-Porter, Design: Neil Korpinen.

p. 69: Photo: © Gail Owens.

p. 70: Photo: © www.davidduncanlivingston.com.

p. 71: Photo: © Eric Roth.

pp. 72–73: Photo: © Tim Street-Porter.

pp. 74–75: © www.davidduncanlivingston.com.

p. 76: Photo: © Steve Vierra, www.stevevierraphotography.com.

p. 77: Photo: © Brian Vanden Brink, Design: Green Company Architects.

p. 78: Photo: © Jessie Walker.

p. 79: Photo: © Mark Samu, www.samustudios.com.

pp. 80–81: Photo: © Brian Vanden Brink, Design: Peter Breese.

p. 82: Photo: © Eric Roth.

p. 83: Photo: © Harrison Design Associates.

p. 84: Photo: © Eric Roth, Design: Frank Roop.

p. 85: Photo: © Eric Roth, Design: Dotty Volpe.

CHAPTER 3

p. 87: Photo: © Jessie Walker.

p. 88: Photo: © Mark Samu, www.samustudios.com, Design: Lucianna Samu.

p. 89: Photo: © Mark Samu, www.samustudios.com.

p. 90: Photo © Tria Giovan.

p. 91: Photo: © Tim Street-Porter.

pp. 92–93: Photo: © Brian Vanden Brink.

p. 94: Photo: © Jessie Walker.

p. 96: (top) Photo: © Eric Roth; (bottom) Photo: courtesy Interiors by Decorating Den.

p. 97: Photo: © Jessie Walker.

p. 98: (top) Photo: © www.davidduncanlivingston.com.

p. 99: Photo: © Brian Vanden Brink, Design: Cornelia Covington Smithwick.

p. 100: Photo: © Steve Vierra, www.stevevierraphotography.com.

p. 101: Photos: courtesy Spring Window Fashions LP.

p. 102: Photo: © Mark Samu, www.samustudios.com.

p. 103: Photo: © Eric Roth.

p. 104: Photo: © Brian Vanden Brink, Design: Scholz & Barclay Architects.

p. 105: Photo: © Jessie Walker, Architect: Thomas L. Bosworth.

CHAPTER 4

p. 107: Photo: © Jeremey Samuelson.

p. 108: Photo: © 2006 Carolyn L. Bates, www.carolynlbates.com

p. 110: Photo: Michael Dunne, courtesy Elizabeth Whiting Associates.

p. 111: (right) Photo: © Randy O'Rourke, Design: Austin Patterson Disston Architects; (left) Photo: Michael Dunne, courtesy Elizabeth Whiting Associates.

p. 112: Photo: © Jason McConathy, Design: Kristi Dinner/KD Design.

p. 113: Photo: © Mark Samu, www.samustudios.com, Design: Douglas Moyer Architect.

p. 114: Photo: © Brian Vanden Brink, Design: Mark Hutker and Associates.

p. 115: Photo: © Mark Samu, www.samustudios.com.

pp. 116–117: Photo: Charles Miller, © The Taunton Press, Inc.

pp. 118–119: Photo: courtesy Diamond Cabinets.

p. 120: Photo: © Brian Vanden Brink.

p. 121: Photo: © Ken Gutmaker.

p. 122: Photo: © Rob Karosis.

p. 123: Photo: © Steve Vierra, www.stevevierraphotography.com.

p. 124: Photo: © Tom Hopkins.

p. 125: Photo: © Ken Gutmaker.

CHAPTER 5

p. 127: Photo: © Ken Gutmaker.

p. 129: Photo: Charles Miller, © The Taunton Press, Inc.

pp. 130–131: Photo: © Rob Karosis.

p. 132: Photo: © Ken Gutmaker.

p. 133: Photo: © Rob Karosis.

p. 134: Photo: © Susan Gilmore.

p. 135: Photo: © Sandy Agrafiotis.

p. 136: Photo: © www.davidduncanlivingston.com.

p. 137: Photo: © Chipper Hatter.

pp. 138–139: Photo: © Rob Karosis.

CHAPTER 6

p. 140: Photo: courtesy The Land of Nod.

p. 142: Photo: © Tim Street-Porter.

p. 144: Photo: © Chipper Hatter.

p. 145 (left) Photo: © Scot Zimmerman; (right) Photo: © Brian Vanden Brink.

pp. 146–147: Photos: © Brian Vanden Brink, Design: Drysdale Associates Interior Designs.

p. 148: Photo: courtesy Peggy Nelson/ www.thepaintedroom.com.

p. 149: Photo: © Mark Samu, www.samustudios.com, Design: Steve Goldgram Design.

p. 150: Photo: © Sandy Agrafiotis, Design: Benjamin Nutter Architects.

p. 151: Photo: © Oscar Thompson, Design: Marc-Michaels Interior Design.

pp. 152–153: Photos: © Sargent 2006, Design: Marc-Michaels Interior Design.

p. 154: Photo: courtesy Pottery Barn.

p. 155: Photo: © Wendell T. Webber.

p. 156: Photo: © www.davidduncanlivingston.com.

p. 157: Photo: © Jessie Walker.

p. 158: Photo: Charles Miller, © The Taunton Press, Inc.

p. 159: Photo: © www.davidduncanlivingston.com.

CHAPTER 7

p. 161: Photo: © Kari Haaviston, Design: Victoria Hagan.

p. 162: Photo: © Brian Vanden Brink.

p. 163: Photo: © Rob Karosis.

p. 164: Photo: © Kari Haaviston, Design: Randy Ridless.

p. 166: Photo: © Rob Karosis.

p. 167: Photo: © Ken Gutmaker.

p. 168: Photo: © Rob Karosis.

p. 169: Photo: © Philip Clayton-Thompson.

pp. 170–171: Photo: © Rob Karosis.

p. 172: Photo: © Philip Clayton-Thompson.

p. 173: Photo: Brian Pontolilo, © The Taunton Press, Inc.

pp. 174–175: Photo: © Chipper Hatter.

p. 176: Photo: © Rob Karosis.